To my mother Erica
who encouraged me to see...

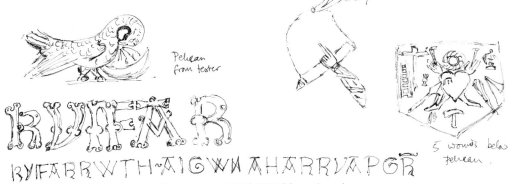

Pelican
from tester

5 wounds below
pelican.

Cotehele: mid 16thC Welsh cupboard

Opposite page: Glendurgan Maze

*Inclusion of a property within this book does **not** mean that it is open to the public, is available to visit, or can be seen from a public right of way. The majority of these buildings are in private occupation. Although one or two may occasionally be open to the public, we emphasise that no property should be considered available for visits and the privacy of owners should be respected.*

ISBN 978-0-9555511-1-6

Printed by R.Booth Ltd. Penryn Cornwall
Published by Pasticcio Ltd   Registered in England No 5125728
www.pasticcio.co.uk

Glendurgan Maze
15·4·95

A Visitor in Cornwall

~ WATERCOLOUR ILLUSTRATIONS OF CORNISH HOUSES ~

Joanna Mattingly
Text: Stephen Tyrrell

A goat from the screen at
Sancreed Church

Introduction

Cornwall has many thousand interesting buildings, from among which we can therefore show only a small selection. Each parish has perhaps twenty large farm or gentry houses hidden down country lanes. Most were built before 1800 and have been little changed since then. Cornwall has remained, despite quarries, clay works and mines, a largely rural area, with a small population spread over a long narrow area. Nowhere is more than thirty minutes from the sea. Although a number of farms had new farmhouses built between 1860 and 1900, there is less Victorian housing than elsewhere, because there has not been that extension of towns and industrial activity that took place up-country. It used to be said that Cornwall relied on fishing, mining and farming, but none of these remains viable. The principal activity of the county is now tourism. The landscape and the appearance of historic houses are therefore all the more important. Most of the illustrations here are of houses on older sites, often picturesque, but seldom visited.

I started painting in watercolours when I was seven. I bought my first box of watercolour paints and sketch pad after a visit to Beatrix Potter's home in the Lake District. Apparently, I was more interested in her amazing Cumbrian landscape backgrounds than in Peter Rabbit or Mrs Tiggiewinkle. Over the next few years, I learnt to paint while on family visits to country houses and had to learn to paint quite fast. Each such visit would start with a race round the house with my brother and sister so that I could get back outside, have a sketch done and the first spot of paint applied before my parents caught up.

Old Town Church, St Mary's, Isles of Scilly

If successful, I would be allowed to spend a bit more time on the sketch. In this way I learnt that most water-colours must be done quickly. An hour or more became delightful indulgence.

Although I am now grown up, it is still a relief to get the drawing done in time. 'Leave some white paper showing' was my mother's advice. I try and leave something to the imagination. Sometimes I stop too soon, or spoil a sketch by doing too much. With watercolour you can't wipe out mistakes. The restric-tions placed on you by Cornish hedgerows and coun-tryside often mean you have to paint from a position too close to houses which have a nasty habit of not fitting on one page. Windows are the eyes of a build-ing and my normal starting point.

I use a ridiculously tiny brush, useless for great swathes of colour but handy for painting in each window pane. I've worn out a lot of brushes but don't use much paint. I still have the Rowney paint box bought when I was 19 and another given to me by Charles Spicer of the Cornish Buildings Group.

The watercolours have never been sketches for larger works, but are ends in themselves, the equivalent of the Edwardian Lady's flower sketches. They remain stuck in sketch books to amuse friends and family.

It was during visits arranged by the Cornish Buildings Group that many of these pictures were done, often in haste while I waited to go in, finishing a sketch just in time to tag on to the end of a tour.

Rhubarb forcing pots and decorative cabbages in the Melon Garden
"THE LOST GARDENS OF HELLIGAN"
2·9·93

Rhubarb Pots, Heligan Gardens

Visiting the houses is fun, as is doing a sketch. This has many advantages over photography, since not only do I retain a visual record of the building to take away, but the slower art of drawing has taught me to look at houses more closely.

As we made a selection for this book, it became clear that there were many omissions. If your favourite house is not included, this may be because I haven't visited it, forgot my paints, didn't feel like sketching, had to help the house tour or found it was pouring with rain.

There are lots of buildings which deserve inclusion. My friends too have argued for their favorites to be seen. As well as historic buildings, we could also have covered a wider range of building types.

This selection has no industrial warehouses, no gasometers, no housing estates, no 19th century chapels, no public buildings.

I can't wait to do a second book and hope that this volume will sell with such enthusiasm that we will be able to do another.

It is traditional to thank those who have helped with the book. Family and friends are thanked for

St James the Great, Gunwalloe
Rood Screen Detail

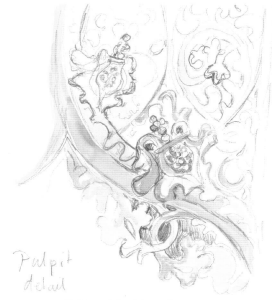

St Mary Magdelene, Launceston

their forebearance, Mark Nightingale for his help with the graphic design.

There is however only one thank you of any importance. This must be to the owners or occupiers of each building.

It is a sad reflection of our times that many owners fear the visitor may represent a bureaucratic authority who could affect their lifestyle or building. A burglar or double-glazing salesman might be more welcome than one of those. Historians too, may be viewed with suspicion. It is the more amazing, therefore, that so many owners have allowed us in, permitted a visit, and indulged our curiosity.

We must emphasise that most of these properties are private, and that any uninvited access or visit is improper.

These watercolours would not have been possible without the generosity of the occupiers, to whom we are grateful.

Map

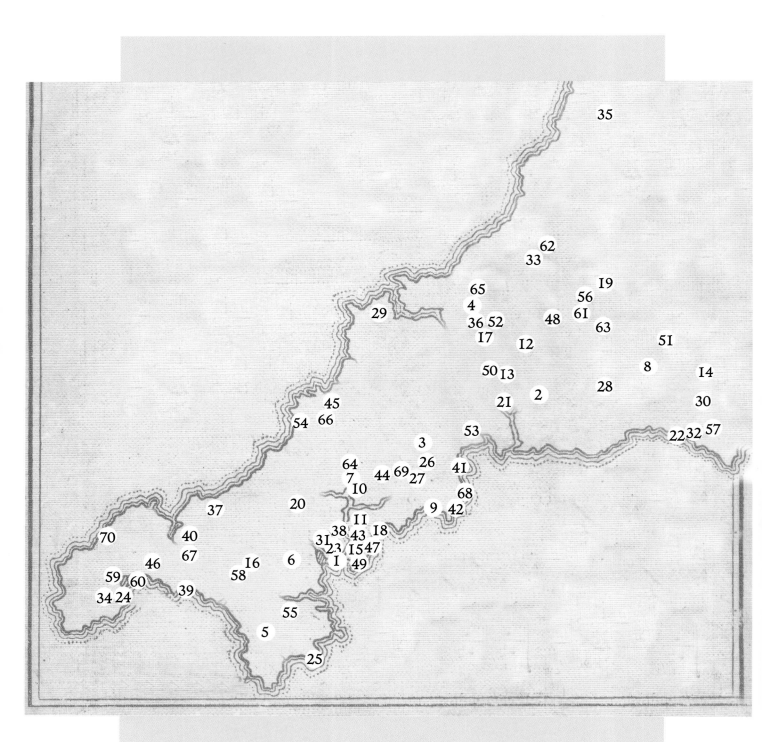

Location Key

1. Arwennack, *Falmouth*
2. Boconnoc House, *Boconnoc*
3. Bodinnick, *St Stephen in Brannel*
4. Bokelly, *St Kew*
5. Bonython, *Cury*
6. Bosvathick, *Constantine*
7. Bosvigo, *Truro*
8. Browda, *Linkinhorne*
9. Caerhays Castle, *Caerhays*
10. Calenick, *Kea*
11. Carclew, *Mylor*
12. Cassacawn, *Blisland*
13. Castle Hill Farm, *Bodmin*
14. Cotehele, *Calstock*
15. Cottage, *St Mawes*
16. Crasken, *Wendron*
17. Croan Manor, *St Mabyn*
18. Crugsillick Manor, *Gerrans*
19. Cullacott, *Werrington*
20. Cusgarne House, *Gwennap*
21. Duchy Palace, *Lostwithiel*
22. Erth Barton, *Saltash*
23. Falmouth Working Men's Club
24. Fisherman's Arms, *Newlyn*
25. Friendship Cellar, *Coverack*
26. Garlenick, *Creed*
27. Golden Manor, *Probus*
28. Halbathic, *Nr Liskeard*
29. Harlyn House, *St Merryn*
30. Hatt House, *Botus Fleming*
31. Hingston's House, *Falmouth*
32. Ince Castle, *Saltash*
33. Kenningstock Mill, *Advent*
34. Kerris Barton, *Paul*
35. Launcells Barton, *Launcells*
36. Lemail, *St Mabyn*
37. Menadarva, *Gwithian*
38. Pandora Inn, *Mylor*
39. Pengersick Castle, *Breage*
40. Penpol, *Hayle*
41. Pentewan, *St Austell*
42. Penwarne, *Nr Mevagissey*
43. Porloe, *Nr Mylor*
44. Probus Church, *Probus*
45. Rialton Barton, *St Columb Minor*
46. Rosemorran, *Gulval*
47. Rosteague, *Gerrans*
48. St Clether Holy Well, *St Clether*
49. St Mawes Holy Well, *St Mawes*
50. St Petroc, *Bodmin*
51. Trecarrell Manor, *Lezant*
52. Tregarden, *St Mabyn*
53. Tregrehan, *St Blazey*
54. Treguth Inn, *Holywell Bay*
55. Trelowarren, *Mawgan-in-Meneage*
56. Treludick, *Egloskerry*
57. Trematon Castle, *Saltash*
58. Trenethick Barton, *Wendron*
59. Trengwainton, *Madron*
60. Trereife, *Penzance*
61. Trerithick, *Altarnun*
62. Trethin, *Advent*
63. Trevadlock, *Lewannick*
64. Trevean, *Kenwyn*
65. Trewane, *St Kew*
66. Trewerry Mill, *Newlyn East*
67. Trewinnard, *St Erth*
68. Trewinney, *Nr Mevagissey*
69. Trewithen, *Probus*
70. Wicca Farm, *Zennor*

Arwennack

Arwennack Manor,
Falmouth 18·6·'96

Arwennack is on low ground just before Pendennis Castle, Falmouth, and was once the strong house at the entrance to the estuary. From 1385, Arwennack was the home of the Killigrews who were merchants, castle defenders, founders of Falmouth, occasional pirates and a family whose history would fill many a romantic novel. The house was being rebuilt when burnt in the Civil War, so the ruined hall may never have been completed. After another fire in 1978, the house was restored by Len and Jill Williams, early supporters of historic renovation. The picture shows Jill Williams' garden with the ruined Great Hall as a back drop.

Boconnoc House

Boconnoc House

Boconnoc House is within the most satisfying landscape. My spirits always rise as I drive through the park, past obelisk, monuments and deer. In the 1400s, the site was known as *The Tower of Boconnoc*. It is still possible to trace the mediaeval courtyards and great hall under 15thC roof trusses. Refaced and extended in the 18thC, Boconnoc lost a wing or two in the 20thC.   It is still a large house in an 18thC landscape, with a mediaeval deer park - and deer - to one side, a 15thC church, stable yards and other fine estate buildings.   As you might expect, there are romantic stories about the house and its owners, their battles, duels, and adventures. After the previous owner lost a duel, Governor Pitt bought the estate in 1716 with the profit of one large diamond. He started a political dynasty, so that the house has been associated with three prime ministers. Boconnoc has remained in that family since then. The last seventy years have not been easy. However, it is good to see the house beautifully repaired and a family home once more. Boconnoc is also a centre for many activities and functions, like that during which this watercolour was done.

Bodinnick

Bodinnick, Combe, St Stephen in Brannel   19·9·04

Bodinnick is outside St Stephen in Brannel and has been a working farm for centuries. The house was rebuilt in 1602 and then extended and again refronted in 1765 by someone whose initials in stone are quite unreadable. Now an organic farm, it has interesting buildings from many centuries. These include a barn of which one wall has fine cut stone, a 6 light granite mullioned window, string course and other remnants from an older house. It is all confusing enough to mystify the expert. Inside, the house has many fine features including a granite paved floor, a cloam oven, hollow chamfer stone mullioned windows and also rather younger 16 and 20 paned sash windows. I remember a surprising 18thC room upstairs, with doors and panelling, and in one of the front rooms a wonderful 1930s brown tile fireplace.

Bokelly

Granary & Barn at Bokelly
St Kew   16.6.96

Bokelly, just north of St Kew may have been a monastic site. The mediaeval house, from which a little stone window survives, was rebuilt around 1615 as a great mansion. Bits of that house can still be traced. William Carnsew's diary from 1576 famously reports visits with his friends at Bokelly. The main house had a 19thC re-modelling. The whole site remains a fascinating conundrum.

One of the wonders and puzzles is the Great Barn just opposite the back door. Built of stone with high thick walls, it is an unusual survivor, rare in Cornwall and built perhaps in the 16th or 17thC to a magnificent scale. The threshing floor, interior space, slate slab roof and stone buttresses are all large and there are many rows of holes for breeding young pigeons or *squabs* for the table. Inside it is one big space. You get a stiff neck from peering up to the roof.

Outside is a rare little pyramidal granary which stands on timber beams on top of staddle or mushroom stones, doing their real job.

Bonython

Bonython
Mawgan in Meneage

Bonython, in Cury on the Lizard, was an important manor for the Bonython family from around 1370 to 1720. In 1790, John Trevenen built this astonishing wing, perhaps to designs of William Wood. The new house with basement and two storeys crosses the end of a mediaeval house modernised in 1600 which still exists as the rear service wing. The 1790 section is only one room thick, but filled with panelling, plas-terwork and other original details. I remember an astonishing staircase. The Bonythons left their mark on many a Cornish house, though the family is now said to be in Australia. In 1867 Bonython was described as 'a modern building, surrounded by considerable thriving plantations'. There are now fine gardens around the house, but that is a totally inadequate description for a house that is one of the most beautiful in Britain.

Bosvathick

Bosvathick, Constantine   6.5.'07

Bosvathick, Constantine, has been lived in by one family since 1760. The Georgian house was built by a survivor from the 1745 rebellion planning a quiet life far from Scotland. Later his family financed privateers, dealt in property, and married well. The house was extended with a mid Victorian porch and a later high ceilinged wing and courtyard built on the site of the demolished Elizabethan house. Bosvathick is a bit of a time capsule, with 19thC interiors and layout but still a working farm and office. Inside it is fascinating. Outside there is a large rambling garden. Bosvathick is home to Collie-dogs who will try and lick you to death while you are painting!

Bosvigo

Bosvigo, Truro   17·9·89

Bosvigo, Kenwyn, is a small country house built and extended round an 18thC core, so that it is now H shaped but with other extensions. Famous owners have included the Scholls and the Lemons. It has starred in the Wycliffe series on TV as if it were a field or two away from Godolphin.

Bosvigo has some early sashes with thick glazing bars and lots of crown glass, and an interior that records decorating fashions across two hundred years. Surviving items include 18thC panelling and later Gothic features. Although only a small country house, there is a ballroom, but I do not know if that is much used.

Browda

Browda, Linkinhorne

Browda in Linkinhorne was rebuilt by the Kittows in 1602 and some of that house remains. The initials R.K. and the date are inscribed on the wainscotting inside. In common with other houses of the period, a two storey porch leads to a wide passage, with two rooms to the left, one to the right and the stair hall at the back. It was much altered and rebuilt in the mid to late 19thC for Thomas Kittow, who was the purser at South Caradon Mine. He seems to have had a good and particularly long life since he lived to be 101 years old, dying here in 1886. The air and life of Cornwall were always held responsible for particular longevity. Long may that continue.

Caerhays Castle

23 · 4 · 2000

Caerhays Castle is unusual in having been built from scratch as a picturesque castellated Gothic style country mansion. JB Trevanion asked Nash to design it and it was built in 1808. Caerhays matches the vision in a demanding Gothic novel. It has a large porte-cochere, towers, Gothic arches, ribbed ceilings and interesting corners and is a statement of English rather than local taste, of aspiration rather than comfort. There's a big service wing, courtyards, walls and a large fine garden. It is said the hill had to be moved (by hand), so that you could see the sea.

Calenick

Calenick 27·11·'88

C alenick, Kea, was rebuilt in 1702 as a fine Queen Anne house in the valley. It belonged to Samuel Enys around 1711, who also built the Old Mansion House in Truro. Close by was an iron smelting works which worked from 1711 until 1891 and for much of this period Calenick acted as the *Count House* to the works. Inside it is little altered, with original features, scantle slate topped walls outside and original windows to the front. The clock tower for the smelting works was built by William Lemon around 1749 and still has the original 1756 clock mechanism by Richard Wallis, with iron slag weights and cast iron hands. Calenick is a house I have always admired.

Finding the Way

The more interesting the house, the more difficult it can be to find. Several houses illustrated in this book are down remote little lanes, on highways once important for the horse, but which were bypassed by the toll roads of the 18thC. Such journeys can be fraught with difficulty. I refer for instance to the map reading of one companion: *'turn right in another inch'*.

One suggested difference between men and women is that women are prepared to ask for directions. This is not always easy. I have never forgotten searching in France for *'Le Camping'*, which I pronounced in five different ways. Each was greeted with blank incomprehension before I finally heard *'Ah, Le Com-pinggg'* as infuriating confirmation of my linguistic inability.

There is one thing to do before you leave home. I was taught that it was vital to use the lavatory before you set out, and that every opportunity should thereafter be used *'because you never know when you will see another'*. Each excursion therefore becomes an anxious leap-frog between wash-rooms, rather like an agonising game of musical chairs.

Assuming we have prepared for the journey, remembered to bring the organisers' instructions and are nearing the goal, it is still possible to go astray. Directions are all important. There are always some in any group who will get lost. 'Sat Nav', a system unknown to me, will, I am told, often direct a driver to a remote and impassable cart track. Indeed, the car of two older ladies recently became bogged far down a narrow track. Some roads have gates, sheep and cattle to negotiate, or will have a tractor blocking the only route. Worst of all, the owners might have forgotten you were coming. Fortunately, they often compensate by proving themselves the friendliest of hosts.

At a house that is difficult to find, you sometimes hear the few who have arrived discuss their journey, adventures and superiority as though they have climbed Everest.

For those who plan to paint, the viewpoint and a comfortable seat are all important. However, it is worth checking before entering the house, that you have not sat or walked on manure.

One recent day-out started badly when I walked the wrong path for a mile or two. Only the dog was delighted. When I finally arrived, there was nothing but mud, mud, glorious mud, and nowhere to sit. The friendly owner then appeared in a chef's hat, which was puzzling until we realised we had found that Cornish Mecca, a farm pasty unit.

We were in the right place.

Mylor Church: Graffiti

Carclew

Carclew
4 July 2007

Carclew, Mylor, was one of the largest houses of Cornwall, a Palladian mansion that is now a romantic ruin. Samuel Kemp began building in the 1720s but ran out of money, so it was extended and finished by William Lemon to designs of Thomas Edwards. The Edwards pavilions were replaced with a library and other great rooms during two further 18th & 19thC extensions and rebuilds. The east end was gutted by fire in 1934 and much of the stone to that end later sold. The enormous portico, west wing and clock tower remain, awaiting rebirth. Now the garden to a house close by, Carclew is a riot of old carved stones, colour and garden enthusiasm.

Cassacawn

CASSACAWN, BLISLAND   17·7·94

Cassacawn, Blisland. This little house is one of three one-up one-down cottages sharing the same well. These were probably built in the early 19th century for farmworkers of the manor house across the road.

The cottage is not particularly grand but a typical survival which has been carefully renovated, and is still not much bigger than when it was built. It belongs to good friends who, as archaeologists, spend much time digging up the deserts of Africa, so coming home to this green place must be a real delight to them.

Castle Hill Farm

Castle Hill Farm, Bodmin   11.9.'98

Tower Hill Farmhouse, Bodmin, is on Castle Hill. It was rebuilt in 1614, then altered in 1700 and through the 18thC. It lies in the shadow of the church tower and still has an old clockwork spit jack for turning meat in the former kitchen. Although the house is interesting, much glory lies in the dilapidated outside buildings, walls, pigsties, apple house, and little 19thC schoolroom. Henry Mudge, the temperance reformer, was born here in 1806. I'd meant to paint the house but this barn, carriage house and stable, with red painted doors and crested ridge tiles, proved irresistible. The carriage house is said to have a mural, pencilled in 1900, showing the fashions of the day.

Cotehele

Cotehele

Cotehele, Calstock, is justifiably one of the best known houses in Cornwall. The survival of the once common hall and courtyard is rare. Stone buildings started around 1300, but much was rebuilt by the Edgcumbe family between 1485 and 1520. The courtyard plan is original. Apart from the building of a mid 16thC tower -for status not defence- and remodelling the east range in 1862, the place is pretty well as it was. There was never a classical makeover. Indeed, it became an 18thC visitor attraction with old furniture and armour brought in. Now, Cotehele is always worth a visit and it helps one understand old houses and layouts elsewhere.

Croan Manor

Croan Manor, St Mabyn
18. 6. 95

Croan in Egloshayle was a 17thC great house owned by the Roscarrocks. Indeed, they admitted to eleven hearths for the 1664 hearth tax, so it must have been quite a place. In 1696, it was rebuilt and extended across the contour lines for Edward Hoblyn. Although bits of the old house may lie to the rear, or have been reused, Hoblyn's house was an early fashion statement for the new architecture. The seven-bay front has heavy glazing bars to the windows. Inside are overmantels with paintings, wall paintings and much 17thC detail. Outside there are old walls, a kitchen garden, two garden pavilions, the remains of a large dovecot and fine drives and landscaping to display the house.

Crugsillick Manor

Crugsillick Manor   18·9·88

Crugsillick Manor, Veryan, is a 17thC house substantially rebuilt in 1710 by the Kempe family, whose most famous descendent was an 18thC admiral. The house has tight enclosing wings. Much of the interior retains the features and appearance given it in 1710. One or two doors, frames and the second stair may survive from the earlier house, but the need to rebuild may have had something to do with the reply of John Kempe to the Hearth Tax in 1664 which reads - '3 (hearths), stopt up, 2 (hearths) & ye house converted to a barn'. That work reduced the tax, but must have made the house uncomfortable. The resultant renovation is now a fine 1710 survival.

Cullacott

English Heritage scaffolding
& protective roof.

Dovecote in barn end

Lower End (unheated)

Cross passage

Open Hall with lateral Fireplace
→ parlour end.

ANNO DO: 1579: BY WATER BLYGHTE

Mullion window head   at parlour end

CULLACOTT
(c1500, 1579, late 17C) 20. 6.'93

Cullacott, Werrington, is a wonder. Much of the rebuild from 1575-9 remains unaltered. It has mullioned windows, high hall, minstrels' gallery, mediaeval religious wall paintings and a dragon breathing fire. The 17thC alterations give a good idea of life at that time. Cullacott is a 'timewarp' house, which has been called the most important surviving mediaeval house in Cornwall. Pretty well abandoned for the last 150 years, it was repaired at enormous cost and care in the 1990s and still under scaffolding when I did this sketch. The final glory of Cullacott must be the money and patience of the farming family who have overseen the renovation.

Cusgarne House

22.9.'02

Cusgarne House

Cusgarne House, Gwennap, may be a 17thC house of which old sections remain to the rear. It was refaced around 1750, and has retained that window facade with much original glass. The interior is little altered and has good panelling and a fine stair in the turret to the rear. This house is famous because it was rented by James Watt between 1781 and 1800 whilst he fitted steam engines to pump water from the mines of Cornwall. The hamlet has an organic farm, a larger manor farmhouse next door and several good late 18th and early 19th century buildings.

Owners

Buildings are often the product of the personality or interests of the owners and of unexpected events. We forget that a building is admired because an earlier owner had stamped his character on the house. It is very difficult to get permission to alter an old building today. Although such restrictions are well-intentioned, it is now almost impossible to replicate that earlier eccentricity that we now value. It is precisely that disparate variety which is so often disallowed. Bring back eccentric owners, say I.

Of these, I have met a variety over the years. Once, arriving for a first meeting, the owner was found at the back peering over the hedge at his neighbour. To me, he did not say 'hello', or 'Who are you?', but complained: 'And another thing, Never trust those B...ers. Cheats all of them.' It was difficult to know what to say. Our conversation was not made easier when he turned slightly to one side, undid his flies and relieved himself, still of course with his head turned to me. It was only later that I discovered the police had just removed his shotgun.

Another owner emphasised that he was 'an entre-PEN-Yawer, an entre-PEN-Yawer', and that everything was of the best, and in the best possible taste. Another man was proud to have and to demonstrate the best in technical excellence and gadgetry.

Others produce magazine pictures and show that a house has been altered to 'look just like that', a habit very much in the tradition of 17th, 18th and 19thC design. I remember a delightful farmhouse where the farmer brought me in from the cowyard with filthy boots, but said 'keep them on', to go upstairs.

Some owners are quieter, greet your comments with a quizzical look. Some give you too much coffee, offer too many theories, or give a long and on occasion unconvincing potted history. Never disagree with an owner who states that his house was built in the 12thC with timbers from the Armada, as the home of Henry VI and his eighth wife. Never disagree with any of their theories. Rather should each proud proprietor be encouraged in his eccentricity, since that may provide an interesting house for future generations.

One thing all visited houses have in common is that most appear tidier, neater and better thought out than mine. Other families lives in beautifully decorated order rather than our jumbled chaos. Walking from room to room between their ornaments becomes a nightmare. Never throw your arms out to demonstrate to your friends an interesting architectural detail.

Owners of interesting houses will all have had visitors who claim to be a third cousin, or say their ancestors owned the house. Some visitors are selling double glazing or a 'free' kitchen. Others just look incredibly suspicious, or might be from the local authority. It is surprising we are allowed into so many houses.

For our hosts, each visit is a patiently endured imposition. We remember these kind people with gratitude.

Landewednack: a lichened angel's corbel

Duchy Palace

Duchy Palace

Duchy Palace, Lostwithiel, was never a palace, but more a grand office, built alongside the river wharves, below the new bridge which allowed Lostwithiel's foundation. The palace was the *Convocation Hall* probably first built in 1280. It is Cornwall's finest mediaeval secular building and lies at the east end of the range from which the Duchy was administered. It seems the Black Prince may have visited in 1353, leaving a plume of feathers carved in the roof. Other buildings include a great hall, weighing house, blowing house, coinage hall, and a prison used by the Stannary Parliament. It is a complex group which will no doubt one day be further researched.

Erth Barton

ERTH BARTON
near SALTASH
19.5.'91

Erth Barton, Saltash, must have been a grand mediaeval manor, until replaced by a 17thC rebuild. There are fine features, a six-light mullioned window, a tower porch and good oak doors. Very unusual is the free standing first floor chapel to the south, entered by stone steps to the side. This is probably a rare 13thC survival, even having remnants of mediaeval wall painting. It has pigeon holes in the gable, round a three-light traceried window. Down below, a cider house still retains its presses. The chapel must have been familiar to Robert Bond who married the daughter of Geoffrey de Erth around 1400. Erth Barton then became the Bond home for 200 years.

Falmouth Working Men's Club

Bell's Court has been the home of the Falmouth Working Men's Club since 1866. Once overlooking the main harbour in the oldest part of Falmouth, the 17thC house was Killigrew's port and tax office. It had an early 18thC makeover, of which many fine details survive. In 1764 it was the home of George Bell, one of three generations of packet agents who lived here, until the offices moved to Custom House Quay in 1814. It was here that the Riot Act was read in 1810 by Christopher Saverland to packet sailors in the *Falmouth Mutiny*, who were arguing about their 'personal' imports. This colonnaded porch is like that at Keigwin, Mousehole. The friendly club is the home of snooker and other sports. The rebuilt section next door has a terrific delicatessen.

Fisherman's Arms

Fisherman's Arms, Newlyn   12·7·07

Fisherman's Arms, Newlyn, has been an inn whose landlords' names are known from around 1810. Possibly 17thC -there is a fine old fireplace- it was altered in the 19thC. The Fisherman's Arms, by the south pier, is a popular traditional pub in the heart of old Newlyn, a town of narrow vertical streets, opes, walkways, and astonishingly ancient houses. The ceiling is festooned with strange things from round the world, and these include three *Puffa fish*.

Friendship Cellar

FRIENDSHIP CELLAR
COVERACK

17·4·'92

Friendship Cellar, Coverack, is a good example of a pilchard pressing cellar or *palace*. Shoals of pilchards were processed during an intensive 6-8 week period each autumn. Vast amounts of salt were used as 'mortar' to make a wall of fish. After a month this was taken down, the fish washed and then pressed into barrels, using stone weights and long levers jammed under a ledge built into the wall. Most of the pilchards were shipped to Italy. An important by product was *train* (fish) oil which was used for lighting and heating. Every port, small or large, had courtyards and ranges of cellars for storage, for handling fish and repairing nets. Many are now holiday homes.

Garlenick

Garlenick, Creed

19·9 '04

Garlenick, Creed, was a gentry house of importance. The Shropshire family of Woolridge lived here from 1554 to the early 19th century and the gateposts, dated 1682, may date from their last refurbishment. In 1812 Gwennap Moore rebuilt the house to the latest fashion, a Regency house with 'Gothick' crenella-

tions, a 'modern' interior and decoration to look at rather than use. It has a fine Regency interior, which includes a chimney piece with crossed guns in memory of Sir John Moore of Corunna. The house is hidden away north of Grampound, in an area with several good and historic houses. How unusual to find at Garlenick a Regency villa in the 'latest' style.

Golden Manor

Golden Manor, Probus
12.9.94

Golden Manor, Probus, has a wonderful name and confused history. More properly *Wolvedon*, this had become *'Golden'* when the tin merchant John Tregian was building the earliest brick house in Cornwall in 1537-1540. Brick walls, other puzzles in the gardens, and *Golden Keep,* a small brick tower, may all be part of that exceptional courtyard house, whose owners suffered for their Catholic faith. Probably demolished to provide bricks for Trewithen, the remaining service wing was refronted in 1631 and 1644 by the family of Ezechiel Grosse, a notorious moneylender. Across the lane, a barn with a solid stone spiral stair turret was part of the 15thC house and then the entrance and chapel court. Behind the 17thC and part 18thC facade, Golden Manor has a 16thC fireplace with mermen, a smiling granite gargoyle and an early herringbone brick fireplace.

Halbathic

HALBATHIC near LISKEARD

26·4·'9:

Halbathic, near Liskeard, is an example of the smaller farm house. Long abandoned when the present owners started work, it had been a mediaeval longhouse where people lived at the higher end and animals at the lower. Rebuilt in the late 16th and 17thC centuries it has been little altered since the 19thC. When Vaughan and Abi started work, the kitchen end had fallen down and the plank and muntin screen was protected by corrugated iron. They uncovered the longhouse drain for animals. One room had been used as Liskeard's earliest Quaker meeting by the Mounce family. It is charming and interesting, and inside are old *keeping places* for lights or knick-knacks.

Harlyn House

Harlyn House
5.7.07

Harlyn, St Merryn, is a large rambling house on a Celtic site. It has been altered again and again. There's a 16thC core altered in 1635 (lovely seabeast plaster), a long wing from 1700 and finally extensions of 1798 and 1820 with dramatic Gothic treatment (friends at Prideaux Place). It includes stones from the destroyed church of St Constantine and the only mediaeval rock anchor I know. It was the home of the Michell and then of the Peters family, whose rents included a limpet pie. Harlyn started to decay 100 years ago and is now being renovated at last. There really is a *haha* in front of the house. Ferocious barking and rain kept me in the car for this picture.

Group Visits

There are many associations in Cornwall for whom house visits are arranged. They include those interested in local history, industrial buildings, Cornish Heritage, Social History, Family History - you name it, an organisation seems to exist. Because of my life as a local historian, I am a member of far too many.

A great favourite is *The Friends Of Glasney*. Glasney, established on a marsh just outside Penryn in 1265, provided education and training for priests. The college, a centre for Cornish language and plays, was dissolved in 1549, a mere 460 years ago. This does not stop *The Friends* who form one of the most interesting and original of history groups. *The Cornish Buildings Group,* on visits with whom most of these drawings have been done, was set up nearly forty years ago. Its members include a core of historians, architects and cheerful amateurs who run events, review planning items, and arrange visits to little known, interesting houses. They too have their range of the eccentric as well as the enthusaistic. It is good that you can assume a visit will be led by a well-qualified member who will talk without notes, and provide guidance to the building.

Like any such collection of enthusiasts, there is what is usually described as 'friendly debate' or, as I prefer to see it, impassioned argument on almost anything that could be called of historic or building interest, including modern architecture. Such debate can, like a good tennis match, be terrific entertainment.

It is useful to practise being in a visiting group.

Cardinham Church: Painted Piscina

First, assume a look of polite interest. Then, be restrained in conversation and do not criticise loudly some element of the hosts' life-style or furnishing. Third, wipe your feet and keep your arms to the side. Envious remarks should be kept quiet, although, in the English tradition, you can make the odd comment in a muted whisper.

Every group is likely to have someone who will ask one of the following questions.

-When was that picture painted? *(A quick look at the frame may help, but a guess is usually accepted.)*
-Where are the loos? *(Either: 'Wait until we leave the house' or 'Down that corridor, third on the left and then second to the right.')*
-Are all these timbers from old ships?
-How long are we going to be here?
-Where do we go next?
-Which film star lived here?
-This is where Nelson stayed on his way to the battle of Waterloo, isn't it?
-Where is the secret tunnel to the church/pub/sea?
-We think we will wait outside.

Such questions are of course never to be expected from the wise members of the Cornish Buildings Group or any other group where so many happy hours have been spent with my friends.

Hatt House

HATT HOUSE
BOTUS FLEMING
19·5·'91

Hatt House, Botus Fleming. Many 18thC owners would modernise by building a new wing on the old house, as happened here, with a double depth early brick house built in 1710 to flemish bond. A smart entrance was made and the central window in this picture was then the front door. Although it is in attractive but plain Queen Anne style outside, there are a lot of fine things inside and many original fittings. The older house, now reduced in size, has fine 16th & 17thC granite, plasterwork and a bit of a cruck truss. The pride and joy is a delightful rare cupboard which has a fluted shell back, shaped shelves, cherub's head, wings and a painted coat of arms.

Hingston's House

Hingston's House
Falmouth

Hingston's House, Falmouth, overlooks Fish Strand Quay where the news of Trafalgar landed in 1805 and from where the commandos left for the St Nazaire raid of 1942. This is in the earliest, 17thC part of Falmouth, then called Smethwick, where Killigrew started developing. The pretty half-house has thick granite walls, is part-slate hung and may be the 17thC rear of a later house. I was on a market stall during The Tall Ships' Race, and did this sketch while we waited for customers. Today, the house has no red paint and is not easily recognisable. Why was it called Hingston's House? Was he a ship's butcher? Madam in a house of ill repute? A ferryman? A ship owner? A shopkeeper? A preacher? Please supply your own suggestion.

Ince Castle

Ince Castle

Ince Castle, Saltash, is a very unusual house by the estuary. It is symmetrically built of brick, an early use for Cornwall, with granite dressings. There are four three-storey once-battlemented towers with walls four foot thick. It was built without a large hall and no main internal stair, and may have copied a Continental *pavillon de plaisir*. The build date in documents is 1653, a carved stone suggests 1540, but the accepted date is 1642. The owner, Sir Richard Killigrew, died in the Civil War. He left the castle to his mistress Jane Hill and her son. It became a farm in the 1850s, decayed, was restored but then suffered in two fires (the last in 1986) and luxuriously restored again. The story of the Killigrew builder having a wife in every tower sounds fanciful.

Kenningstock Mill

KENNINGSTOCK
MILL, ADVENT
17. 10. '93

Kenningstock Mill, Advent, was one of many Camel Valley mills. The present mill is from the 18th and 19thC, but the 17thC mill and millpond had been just behind it. Perhaps earlier mills had stood before that, fed by the waters rushing down from the moor. Elsewhere, I've been able to trace a mill moving down the valley four times as wheel technology changed from stream bed sited, to undershot, then breast shot and at the last, to the overshot wheel. Most ground grain was barley, or *grist*. This type of mill did not often survive much beyond the mid 19thC.

Kenningstock was restored by architects Mike and Inette Austin-Smith for their retirement, keeping water power for electricity. I remember a house with trout, turbines and wonderful meals.

Kerris Barton

Kerris Manor 6·10·'96

Kerris Barton, Paul, is a courtyard house. In the late 16thC, the Chivertons lived here. Their black servant *Alexander the Moor* was baptized aged 21 in the ruins of Paul church after the Spanish Raid of 1595. Lydia Hicks, daughter of a 17thC owner, married Nowell Tonkin, a Newlyn fish merchant. Amazingly, 15 of her business letters from 1702 to 1718 survive.

After his father bought Kerris in 1694, Richard Pearce added a new front in 1721. The back has earlier and granite features and the front range the typical bolection mouldings and fittings of 1721. Sadly, the renovation may have caused the bankruptcy which followed in 1743.

Prehistoric remains around this old place include the *Roundago* not far away.

Launcells Barton

Launcells Barton

19 9 '98

Launcells Barton, Launcells, had been owned by Hartland Abbey and used as a cell of Austin Canons. After the Dissolution, the Chamond family bought it in 1553. It was later leased by the Call family. Clearly an old house, two ranges survive from the 1600 rebuild. Sir John Call added a posh front between 1765 and 1777 for his sister Jane, who had married the reverend of the parish. It is a big double depth extension with granite quoins and brick dressings and a first floor stone porch. Sir John Call, having made his fortune as an engineer in India, became High Sheriff of Cornwall. He spent ages trying to trace his ancestry back to the Danes.

Lemail

Lemail, St Mabyn 18 6 '95

Lemail, Egloshayle, is a late 18thC house, built on an important site that got a mention in the Exeter Doomsday. The place name comes from *Nansmail,* the valley where 'Mail' lives. There is a fine water mill below the house. Built by the Tremayne family, the house is double depth and reflects much of the architectural fashion of the 1780s. In the 19thC the Tremaynes sold the house to a farmer, and then bought it back 100 years later. The floor plan is typical of this and later houses, and has a central stair to the rear lit by a large round headed window. The attic floor may have been added in the 19thC. Would it look nicer without it? Discuss.

Menadarva

Menadarva   4. 7. 07

Menadarva, Camborne, is on a sheltered plateau by the Red River, just in from the coast where the invading Irish saint warriors landed. The buildings are a mystery. There is a Tudor/17thC farmhouse, with fine grained and painted 18thC panelling. The Tudor hall has one of the largest early fireplaces in Cornwall. Other buildings include the barn of late 16thC mullions, either the wing of a great house or a partially rebuilt folly. The house was left by Jack Arundell, builder of Trerice, to his eldest, favourite, but bastard son. Was this house of similar magnificence? Northwest of the house there are intriguing mounds which might be gardens or buildings. Menadarva was inherited by a small child lost in Spain, so it took a decades long *Bleak House* lawsuit to establish ownership. The ruined estate was taken by the Bassetts. It has been a working farm for 150 years and the family now provide farm-cooked pasties. Menadarva is a magical house and one of my favourite houses in Cornwall.

Pandora Inn

PANDORA INN
RESTRONGUET
7/8/'92

Pandora Inn, Restronguet, was a farm paying the good rent of 8s 4d in 1488. Until the turnpike between Truro and Falmouth opened in 1828, the river was an important short cut and so the house became an inn. First called *The Passage House*, and then *The Ship* it was, around 1800, renamed *Pandora* in memory of the ship unsuccessful against the *Bounty* mutineers. Although a 17thC thatched building (perhaps two houses?), it has been much rebuilt and extended. It retains great indefinable atmosphere, a magnificent seaside position, and humbling low headroom. Fresh crabs can be caught and consumed here, perhaps by the huge rusting anchor outside.

Sketching

Sitting down to a watercolour should be a lonely job. Although occasionally in quiet solitude, many are sketched with other interested people around you, all anxious to make a contribution, or just be friendly. You get used to the nervousness of the sidelong look, the pause as a stroller tries to think of something intelligent or encouraging to say. Some take an apparently relaxed stance two paces behind you, too far to see what you are drawing, but close enough to ensure unease in the artist. Answering helpful comments has never been a strength. Concentration and a wide smile are essential elements for drawing. If we ever meet, please don't ask: 'Have you finished that bit, then?' It upsets me.

A Bench End from St James the Great, St Levan

Not all onlookers are human. Cows can be unsettling. After a family picnic, my family returned to find cows had swooped down to stand round my stool. I know the cows were interested in what I was doing and not in the least critical, but it was unnerving. The laughter of the family did not help.

Sometimes conditions are against you. Rain has sent me rushing to sit in the car, which is comfortable.

My dog may be bored, and I am sorry for him, but delighted to have the shelter and access to my bag of big biscuits or cookies. These are a must for all occasions. I can sit munching and thinking for hours.

Home-made Cookies

Because there is so little to carry, it is easy to get started on a drawing. It is silly, therefore, that water for the paints is sometimes forgotten. When looking at 18thC houses in Essex, in America, we could not find any water, despite sitting on a river jetty surrounded by the stuff. It was fortunate that a nearby brewery party offered free beer, so beer was what was used. It looks fine.

A visit may become an event. I remember arriving at one place, sketch pad ready, to see a solitary honeycomb by a car. 'Swallows playing croquet' said the bee lady complete with veil and smoke gun. 'Weather disastrous for honey and by the time it improves (if it does), brambles will have stopped flowering'. As well as low-flying swallows around the croquet hoops, Brandy, our muddy dog, would rush up every few minutes from different directions, intent on making his mark on my painting. When I removed the painting to safety, he rolled on the paints instead.

Pengersick Castle

15.18.'99

Pengersick, Breage, is one of the few castle looking places in Cornwall. Now thought to date from the 1540s-60s, it was built by the architects of the coastal defences, partly against raiders and thieves but also for status. It has a low gun loophole like those at Polruan. The Millitons who lived here were governors of St Michael's Mount but when William M died in 1556 the estate was divided among seven daughters. Disaster and decline followed. The grounds are full of puzzles. Angela Evans and her family have been devoted carers of this splendid tower and building, maintaining the contents and atmosphere so even cobwebs may go back to the 16th century. Not only their home but a place for events that include ghost hunts.

Penpol

Penpol, Hayle
6. 7. 97

Penpol, Hayle, was rebuilt in the 16thC and then remodelled and extended regularly. Much remains from each period, including a 17thC stair tower. The extensions are perhaps a result of so many changes in occupier. Home of the Penpols, Penpol was owned by the Godophins until 1639, then sold to Honeychurch, then Robartes, then Curnow, Hocken and in 1788 Richard Miller bought it from the Arundells. A later Dr Miller was found innocent of poisoning his brother by adding aconite to horseradish. The Ellis family, who are among the less well known founders of the port at Hayle, have been owners since 1921. The glorious gardens have a ship's figurehead.

Pentewan

Pentewan 25·6·89

Pentewan, St Austell, was renowned for the carvable stone found round here. Mediaeval quarries worked from the cliffs. This rather awkward picture of the Terrace, Church Row, is of five houses built for sea captains in 1821. They are all slightly different, are of stucco and reused 16th/17thC granite quoins and one has a Venetian window. All five are set behind a full length colonnade of Tuscan columns. The terrace was built above the port whose granite walls are now silted up. Off to the right is the church also built in 1821 of Pentewan ashlar with a central coved bay. This was intended to be the centrepiece of a dramatic and original crescent, sadly never finished.

Penwarne

Penwarne

Carved shield and date stone
by back door

near Mevagissey
(south of)

690

Penwarne, Mevagissey, is a long building with later rear wings. To the right of a fine stone porch are double height mullioned windows which once lit a mediaeval hall. The rear, with modern water tank, has a cusp decorated old window, a stone escutcheon and datestone -1640- which may be part of a renovation, or have come from elsewhere. Penwarne was long owned by reserved farmers whose shyness kept this fascinating, important house an unknown mystery. John Carew, son of the famous Richard, once owned the house. At the siege of Ostend in 1601, young Carew lost his right hand to a cannon ball and so then had a wooden hand worked by springs.

Porloe

PORLOE, near MYLOR   18·4·'92

Porloe, Mylor, was built before 1794 for Thomas Braithwaite, a packet captain and 'rough seaman of Herculean proportions'. Packet ships took the mail to far-flung parts of the world and could bring their captains and owners great wealth. This double depth classical mansion on a small scale, with old fashioned wide casements, is exceptional. Inside and out, it is little altered, with original thick glazing bars, plaster and joinery. An old pane is scratched with *Mary Kelly, July 11th, 1820.* I liked the walls downstairs stencilled with green foliage and discovered by John and Liz Bonython. Tales of secret passages to the creek should be taken with a strong pinch of sea salt.

Probus Church

Probus

Probus Church is a 15thC building and a tribute to the competitive instincts of a wealthy parish. The tower, begun in 1523, is the tallest and finest (123 feet 6 inches) in Cornwall, though of Somerset design. Building work resulted in a quarrel between John Tregian of Golden and his brother-in-law Nicholas Carminow.

Parishioners were ambushed by Carminow's men as they returned with stone from the quarry. Datestones in the wall remind us of works done in 1637 and 1768. The 19thC saw the church benefit, or suffer, depending on your point of view, from renovations carried out by G.E. Street in 1850 and then by St Aubyn in 1904.

Rialton Barton

Rialton, Manor, St Columb Min

Rialton Priory, St Columb Major, was a 15thC house belonging to Bodmin Priory. You could say that this was the start of Newquay as a holiday resort. The Priors of Bodmin holidayed here, enjoying hunting, shooting and fishing rather than bucket and spade. Prior Vivian added the posh porch room. Some stained glass from here is now at Trelowarren. The house was once approached through three gateways. Though reduced in size, Rialton still retains much of the old core, the very high status timber and stonework and an astonishing presence. The holy well still stands near the front door, and a modern road rushes past the hill above.

Food and travel

Enjoying food and drink in the car or having a picnic is meant to be pleasure. It is an important English ritual, although not always comfortable. I find it difficult to sit sideways on a rug. I have never mastered any look of posed elegance, and usually manage only angular and wobbly discomfort.

Small folding chairs, if accurately assembled, will put one leg down a hole and throw you to the ground. Ants, wasps, and sloping surfaces all conspire against you.

Retreating to the car is often best. I do miss those walnut drop shelves you could use in the back seat. The modern pull out mug holder is not the same, no matter how many there are.

In order to protect us during crashes, modern cars do not have shelves or rubbish bins. Bring back level shelves with neat upstands, say I.

A good fast meal is probably fish and chips. The car may smell a bit, but less food seems to get into the cracks. I do not recommend Doner Kebabs with salad, or the fashionable large filled rolls. The food goes everywhere, and no one can see your face. Crisps, biscuits and cake are an absolute killer, with crumbs throughout, particularly if there are children in the car. Ice cream will always drip and mark your clothes in embarrassing places.

The best start is to spread newspaper everywhere, open a large rubbish bag and only then get out the food.

Some people have hampers, wicker objects designed to impress, with plates fitted into the lid, and a large space just too small for any useful object. When you open the lid, the weight of plates throws the lid right back and empties the contents on the ground. A hamper suggests style, with white damask napkins and a butler. That experience has never come my way. More likely are several plastic bags full of stuff, including a thermos or two, and those dreadful plastic cups that unify the taste of all substances.

Huge Paper Strawberries decorate an American restaurant for Mother's Day

A thermos is a great standby. I am told you can get wide topped food thermi, but can not see that that would work. How will you persuade the food out?

The principal handicap of thermi is that they break. Once I broke three, on three visits, one after another.

The *Volcano Kettle* shown here is an alternative. It has two thin skins with water between, and claims to boil a pot of tea using just one sheet of the old Times newspaper. Fondly and well remembered, this is a lot of fun. It is also a good way to start a cooking fire.

Rosemorran

Rosemorran, Gulval — longest thatch m

Rosemorran, Gulval, is said to have the longest thatched roof in Cornwall. The house is on an early site, and incorporates much old stonework, including some stones so large it is difficult to work out how masons could have raised them. The rear elevation shows evidence of many changes, including the addition of the stan-dard late 17thC stair tower. Its present character and appearance were achieved through alteration in the late 18thC as a *cottage orne* by the Johns family, so it is very pretty. Many Chinese, Gothic or unusal features have been added to what had once been a granite and cob farmhouse with animals at one end.

Rosemorran

Cornwall but not Devon! (window heads modernised)   14·7·02

The interior has a chinoiserie door and other purposefully quaint details. In 1868 it was described as 'one of the greatest ornaments to the neighbourhood'. However there is more to Rosemorran than this. West of the house are granite ashlar gate posts. South of the house are delightful gates of serpentine plan with acorn caps and spiral moulding, so that each pier, which could be mistaken for a pineapple, in fact looks more like a chess piece. Nearby are the remnants of gardens surrounded by high cob walls. There is also much cut granite work, some of which has been reused in a stable. It looks as though here, or near here, must once have been a magnificent building.

Rosteague

Rosteague 18·9·'88

Rosteague, Gerrans, was 'The leading place in the parish' in 1868, but had long been a fine house. The mediaeval house was extended and refaced in 1700 when it was the Kempe family home, and much decorative work including plasterwork survives. In 1820 it was extended for the Harris family and the thatched summer house may date from their time. Their sedan chair door, showing the Harris arms of three crescents, is now on display in the Royal Cornwall Museum. The house, which belonged to the family of *Mr Rosteke,* from c1400 to c1560, had a chapel. Despite centuries of change, Rosteague is full of good, satisfying details from each period.

St Clether

St Clether
Holy well and chapel
9. 4. 95

St. Clether chapel and holy well, St Clether, lie below a rocky tor half a mile down the valley from the parish church. The well is only a few feet away from the chapel which is joined to it by an underground channel. The well has a granite slab roof over massive stones. Both were rebuilt in the 15thC, and restored in 1897 by Revd. Sabine Baring Gould. The well water runs under the altar to a reservoir in the south wall, as in the text of *Ezekiel XLVI* and was perhaps used to cure lame people. The chapel, 11ft by 20 ft, is smaller than most mediaeval chapels. A rare and delightful survivor, this well chapel with its spring must have been typical of many.

St Mawes

St Mawes holy well and 1 and 3 Grove Hill *hanging baskets more garish
(glazing bars thinner and brick darker red in colour*) 7. 8. '94

St Mawes or *St Mauditus* was the saint of this small wayside mediaeval well, which it is now all too easy to miss as you walk by.

It is said that St Mawes was a schoolmaster saint and that he had here a stone chair (like that of the saint Germoe). To the left of the well is 'Holywell Cottage', which may have reused some walls of the mediaeval well chapel.

Above the well to the right are two brick show houses (long since altered to three cottages) which were built around 1830 on an awkward steep site. The red brick forms a good contrast with the rendered rubble base and surrounding stone work. I like the late 19thC attic.

St Petroc

ST PETROCK'S CHURCH
BODMIN
1469-72 South aisle   17. 7. '94

St Petroc, Bodmin, was the parish church opposite the powerful priory of Bodmin. Some Norman work remains but it was largely rebuilt in 1469-72. Richard Richow was one of the masons who built the south and north aisles. A parchment record of the work was found in the second floor room above the porch. These records make it one of the best documented churches in the British Isles. The church was restored and altered in the 19thC. There is lots to look at including the 12thC ivory relict box that may have held the saint's bones. St Petroc's was part of a powerful administrative complex and is today the largest church in Cornwall. Measuring 150 foot in length, it had a spire of the same height until 1699. Note the old well at the west end.

Trecarrell Manor

TRECARRELL MANOR
20.6.93

Trecarrell Manor, Lezant - Did the baby son and heir really drown in the bath water? Trecarrell was intended to rival Cotehele, but when Henry Trecarrell died in 1544, he left only daughters. After his death, the project was abandoned when the hall was complete. The mediaeval house to the left was refronted by the Manatons in the 17th century. There is also a detached mediaeval chapel. The great hall, with carved stone and heraldic detail, was still not floored when Charles I stayed here in 1644. It must have been draughty since the loose-fit glass to the windows cannot have been there. It was a barn for centuries, then restored as a hall fifty years ago.

To make Portable Soop

Portable Soop is not a misprint for potable or drinkable *soop*, but a type of dehydrated meat chiefly remembered because it was <u>not</u> potable. Also known as *pocket soop* or *veal glew*, this dried liquid was used by the Royal Navy from 1756, and by many an expedition or voyager. Now famous in literature for its horrible glue-like taste, it was nutritious and common until canned meats were invented at the beginning of the 19thC. If you are going to try and cook it, the key is to ensure there is no fat, or it will go rancid. You should reduce the food to a form of jelly. You may also want to leave it out near an oven to dry, before putting it away in the paperbags. It should not be stored in a humid place. If properly made it is said to last for years.

Please let us know how you get on.

Panera's Soup'n' Bread
The Cornish Pasty is famous for providing vegetables and meat in a handy pastry pocket, so making lunch in the mines, fields or else-where an easy, nourishing affair.

An American snack fills a sour dough loaf with lovely black bean soup. The crusty plug cut out of the loaf can be fitted back so that you have a transportable soup in an edible bowl.

'Take a leg of veal and an old cock, skin the cock, and take all the fat from that and the veal, put to them twelve or fourteen quarts of water, a very little whole white pepper and mace, but no salt; (you must skim your pot exceeding well before you put in the spices). Let all these boil together till the meat is quite a mash, the water wasted to about three pints or two quarts, and the liquor exceeding strong; when you think it is enough strain it into a stone bowl thro' a pretty fine fair-sieve, let it stand all night, then clear off all the top and bottom as you do calf's foot jelly, and boil the pure part of the liquor till it be so strong a jelly, that when it is cold, the fire will harden, and not melt it; when you think it enough pour it into tea-cups, about two table spoon-fuls in a cup; let it stand all night; the next morning turn out the little cakes upon a pewter dish, and set them before the fire; if they run you must boil them higher; if they dry they are enough: You must keep them in a paper bag, where there is a fire, as damp will dissolve them.

N.B. The first boiling should be in an iron pot; the secund in a clean scoured brass pan.'

Lunch at Panera's

Tregrehan

Tregrehan

29 4 2001

Tregrehan, St Blazey, although rebuilt in 1689 (the date on an original attic fireplace) is older than it looks. Bodrugans and Edgcumbes preceded the Carlyons who remodelled it in 1706. It was rebuilt by architect William Wood in the 18thC and then again in 1848/9 by architect George Wightwick.

In 1867 Tregrehan was described as 'almost rebuilt within the last twenty years' and with 'a pleasant south-eastern prospect' of land and sea.

Inside, fine features survive from each of the building phases, including the oldest, perhaps a very early double pile build. It has lovely interesting attics. Outside, the famous planned gardens are full of ornaments and good things, and now visitable. A.L. Rowse's mum worked here.

Treguth Inn

16·6·95

Treguth Inn, Holy Well Bay

Treguth Inn, Holywell Bay, Cubert, is a thatched, slate rubble and cob farmhouse which although claimed as 13thC was probably built in the 17thC, with a couple of extensions since then. Although much altered in recent years, Treguth retains the overall height and proportions of that original house. Thatch and its steeper pitched roof remains rare in Cornwall, although once much more common. Early roofs might be of gorse as well as straw or reed. Thatch historians get excited about the surviving underlayers. Here at Treguth we shouldn't worry, but admire the quaint building, the enormous vent-axia and enjoy the beer.

Trelowarren

TRELOWARREN - Gothick Chapel   13.9.'89

Trelowarren, Mawgan-in-Meneage, is justifiably called a *Great House with Chapel*. The Vyvyan family has owned and occupied the house for 450 years, having arrived in Cornwall, so legend says, when their land was swallowed by the sea. The mediaeval core was remodelled in the 17thC and the chapel licensed in 1636. Later alterations reflect 18thC *Strawberry Hill Gothic* and 19thC changes. The chapel and part of the house are now occupied by a Christian foundation. Trelowarren has many fine rooms, windows, courtyards and stonework.   Gates celebrate the 1660 restoration of Charles II. The surrounding estate is ancient and atmospheric.   It is easy to believe that Trelowarren and its family must have been the subject of an hundred romantic novels.

Treludick

Treludick, Egloskerry

5·7·07

Treludick, Egloskerry, is a lovely 16thC house, which looks over an empty green valley. The entrance front, behind granite posts and railings, has a fine stone porch. Inside are some extraordinary survivals - a 1600 decorative ceiling, fine panelling and a 19thC farm kitchen with bench and table. Alterations in the 16thC and 17thC by junior relatives of the Barons of Tregeare have left an historian's puzzle. In the 18thC a new wing included a large first floor room for meetings and hunting parties. Since then, with the exception of new stone barns, little has been altered since 1755. It has now been in the same farming family for over a century. The rolling slate roofs in this back view give some idea of the early add-ons and complexity of Treludick. I find that the back of a house, although sometimes ignored, is often more revealing than a splendid front.

Trematon Castle

FIREPLACE
TREMATON CASTLE
GATEHOUSE (2nd floor)

19.5.'91

Trematon Castle, Saltash, was one of few great castles in Cornwall. There is a shell keep on a mound, a long bailey curtain wall without towers built around 1100, and a fine gatehouse. This 13thC hooded fireplace was one of two in the gatehouse to keep the guards warm. A similar fireplace survives at Carminow in Mawgan-in-Meneage. The castle became part of the Duchy of Cornwall in 1337, remained a strong point, became a prison, and briefly held the treasures of Sir Francis Drake. A house was built in the castle bailey in 1808 for the surveyor general of the Duchy. Some of the bailey wall was demolished so that the tenant could see the sea.

Trenethick Barton

Trenethick Barton
near Helston

23 5 '99

Trenethick Barton, Wendron, quite justifies its grade I listing. The house is large with two wings to the rear, and more hood moulds over the windows than corn in a field. The Seneshalls were here in the 11thC. The Hills, gentry landowners and tin merchants, took over in 1392 and later built a unique granite strong room on the first floor. The house, mostly built or extended in the late 16thC, has an astonishing interior, including a solid stone stair and another with fine newels. It has been little altered since the 18thC, perhaps because it was an un-noticed working farmhouse.

For status, a fine, but purely decorative 16th century gatehouse clearly says 'keep away'. Trenethick is stuffed full of interest, inside and out.

Trengwainton

Trengwainton 6. 7 '97

Trengwainton, Madron, the great house of the Cowling family, was sold in the 17thC and *'The last Arundell of Menadarva almost rebuilt the mansion, and made it his place of residence.'* In 1810, Sir Rose Price, whose money came from Jamaican sugar plantations and slavery, bought and rebuilt the house. The Bolithos bought the 'commodious and interesting mansion' in 1867. The next Bolitho demolished and rebuilt much of the house in 1881/7, although some older parts may have been kept. The house is in prestigious style with a *large Tuscan distyle-in-antae closed porch* - a phrase which is double-dutch to me. T.R. Bolitho also started the gardens. These, with plants found in Assam and Burma, now form an exceptional plant and rhododendron collection.

Trereife

TREREIFE

Trereife, near Penzance, was the home of the Nicholls family, yeoman farmers, gentry and lawyers before the Nicholls widow married the younger literary Le Grice in 1799. Their descendants still live at the house. Described as *'One of the oldest seats in the parish'*, early history is of marriage and alteration. The surviving house with some 17thC remains is one of the most satisfying of Queen Anne designs. The Georgian stables and intervening rooms now form a further but often overlooked wing. There are fine gates, gardens with tall yew hedges and a lovely mellow front that helps define the term *patina*. I think Trereife has, deservedly, starred in several films.

Trerithick

12.7.07

Trerithick, Altarnun

Trerithick, Altarnun, must have been an important courtyard house when John Hicks rebuilt it in 1575, although his son, as is often the habit with sons, changed and altered it all over again. The house, probably both *counting house* and farm, may have had merlons and battlemented eaves to define its status. The 18thC saw considerable alteration and much old stone confusingly used in a barn, before a Gothic redesign in the 19thC. Like many such houses, you can spend hours assessing its history. When the initials and dates *ANNO DOMYNY 1575 BY IOHN HECKS* or *AN DM 1585 BY M+IH* were carved in granite on window or porch, it was a family home. It still is.

Trethin

TRETHIN, ADVENT

17. 10. '93

Trethin, Advent, is a Tudor house renovated and given a new porch early in James I's reign. The parlour wing was added in 1655. Trethin was a quality house for the minor gentry and has not been much altered. Leased by the Rolle family to a branch of the Vivians, Matthew Vivian's initials are on the hood moulds of a window and over the fireplace. The 1664 hearth tax records at least six hearths and two ovens here. The house inventory and Matthew's will from 1664 have also survived, so that it is possible to get some idea of furnishings and life style for a house of that time.

Trevadlock

Old Shoe found in fireplace at
Trevadlock, Lewannick with remains
of leather lace and toe hole cut out

10.10.99

Trevadlock, Lewannick, is a large manor house in the fertile valley east of Bodmin Moor. The older section is 16thC and has many Tudor features and mullioned windows. A large new wing was added in the 17thC and then this wing was partly refaced in the 18thC and the house turned round. The house retains much of its 17th century layout and features. This old shoe was found during renovation. Old shoes were, like *witch bottles*, used as defence against witchcraft and so often hidden in fireplaces or walls in the 17thC. Unlike other clothing, shoes were said to retain human form. Northampton Museum has an index of similar finds from all over the country.

French tart

More Food

It is not often you must face reality and recognise your own failings.

Only when going through the sketch books and diaries of the last twenty years did my weakness become clear. These sketch books have pictures of houses, of churches, of people, of architectural detail, and landscape. Then, burning like a beacon on the hill top, are the pictures showing food.

Trips to see a house, to take a holiday, to visit friends, are often recorded by a picture of the meal, and usually by a drawing of sweet trimmings rather than base necessities. There are no pictures of steak pie, goulash or other 'sensible' meals.

For a hedonist, there is as much pleasure to be got from admiring a meringue as there is in eating the spinach, beans and broccoli that children are taught should be of importance.

There is a practical side.

Travelling in a car or taking a picnic both require food that can be picked at by hand, that is easy to carry, and does not need a table.

Many of these sugary confections can be described as 'Danish Pastries'.

This is a term we used as children to describe the extra bits, the luxury, those morale boosting small pleasures for which

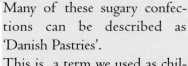

money must be found no matter how broke you are. Here are shown some fast foods for house visits including a massive meringue with clotted cream, ice cream, apple and blackberry, decorated with moulded wafers.

There is a French tart, a picture of delicious little sushi mouthfuls, a cup of coffee with crepes and this little white meringue.

Despite sweet luxury, we remain trim, more like giraffes than hippopotomi. This is because the best meal is often the simplest.

Some bread, a piece of cheese, some cider or a glass of wine remain the most satisfying of pleasures.

They are also practical sustenance to take in a car.

Trevean

TREVEAN
KENWYN 30·6·'94

Trevean, Kenwyn, is immediately south of Kenwyn church. The name suggests an old site, but I think this is the largest and most substantial house in a late Victorian or Edwardian development, where each house has old Cornish names. Trevean is a double pile house with a mass of extensions, window bays and varied archi-tectural detail, built at a time when servants were kept severely separate. This house caught my eye because of its chimneys and blue painted windows. Today wooden window frames are painted white or are just kept as stained wood, a fashion that I abhor. Unless of oak or just left to decay, windows always used to be painted, but not often in white.

Trewane

Trewane, St Kew

Trewane, or Trewarne, St Kew, is fascinating. Bits of an earlier house on a possible monastic site turn up in the garden. The 15thC battlemented tower remains. The house had a high status rebuild when in 1635 the Nicholls son married a Mohun daughter from Boconnoc. Daddy's money probably helped out-splendour all Cornwall, giving Trewane decorated front gables like Trerice, extra big transomed mullioned windows, and rear service wings to leave the front clear. The large rooms were decorated with stories in plaster like those at Lanhydrock or Prideaux Place. Some plaster survives. There is also a little gatehouse. Is this original or a folly? Trewane is one of the most astonishing 17thC houses. Even better, the owners don't seem to mind my jokes.

Trewerry Mill

TREWHERRY MILL
(Trerice manor mill)

29.5.'94

Trewerry Mill, Newlyn East, is inscribed below the string course with *1639 IA MA*, probably the date of an early rebuild by John Arundell of Trerice, for which this was the manor mill. Such mills usually ground barley or *grist* for coarse bread. Trewerry had further rebuilds in 1690 and 1820 when the spandrels were re-cut with *April 10th 1820 Ferrell*. The mill worked until around 1948 but was then converted to a dwelling. An overshot cast iron 16ft wheel is outside and the pit wall is now in the living room. Trewerry is always a good place to paint while waiting for one of Cornwall's best cream teas or for a ghost train at Trewerry Halt, by the long closed railway.

Trewinnard

Trewinnard, St Erth

5 . 8 . '01

Trewinnard, St Erth, retains some remarkable 16thC stonework and a re-sited oriel window from its time as the home of the Trewinnard family. Early in the 18thC the Hawkins family took over, remodelled and re-built the front. Little has changed since then. Inside are fine period features - panelling, fireplaces, doors, cornices and original hangings. The main

door has a shell hood. The wall bears a fire insurance plaque, rare when fire engines are far away. The 18thC stables held the 17thC Hawkins coach, bought from the Spanish Ambassador, used until 1777, and now in Truro Museum. The coach only trundled the Hawkins family to church. This journey of about a mile happened twice each Sunday in the 1750s. Now that is stately one-up-manship.

Trewinney

Mullion window
detail

Trewinney, near Mevagissey

17.5.98

Trewinney, near Mevagissey, is another perplexing house. There was a Tudor farmhouse here, under a steep roof which may once have been thatched. The 18thC rebuild has disguised much, but many interesting features remain, including single skin partitions with crude timber panelling. There is a fine oak mullioned window, typical of 1620 or earlier. I remember puzzling over the building phases and site history. To get into the garden, CBG members had to squeeze past me as I admired the sky reflected in the panes of old glass. It was at Trewinney that our hosts, then going through a Japanese phase, gave us, with generous impulse, an unexpected tea.

Trewithen

Trewithen

18 . 9 . 94

Trewithen, Probus, is one of the finest early 18thC houses in Cornwall. Philip Hawkins, son of the wealthy lawyer from Trewinnard, bought Trewithen and started work around 1715. His cousin and heir Thomas added more to designs of Thomas Edwards in 1738. It was completed to designs by Sir Robert Taylor 20 years later. Trewithen is famous for the quality and extant of very early brickwork, and for being one of few rich men's piles of the time that has not been devastated by fire. Thomas Hawkins' London-born wife Ann was responsible for much of the finery inside. Thomas oversaw the setting out of the grounds, the two detached pavilions in brick, the gates, the brick walled garden. In 1904 a later generation extended and developed the gardens. These may be admired for themselves and for the setting they provide to the house.

Wicca Farm

Wicca Farm
Zennor

14.7.02

Wicca Farm, Zennor, is unusual in that it seems to have been re-built in the early 17thC to house three families in different wings. Wicca reminds us of the difficulties of farming in exposed places, and of the site's long history with massive stones, prehistoric megaliths for neighbours, and fields of granite. The group of buildings seems little altered. Even the through passage remains. There is a big-stoned long grid stile, with seat ledge. The granite-built outside WC has a pyramidal slate roof. We should pay more attention to the survival of those important closets in which so much time is spent. Wicca is a traditional Cornish dairy farm run by the Nankervis family. Osmunda, one of their cows, appears on a kneeler in Zennor church.

Zennor, Penwith

Date Guide

Buildings are ordered by the principal surviving phase shown in each drawing.

Index of drawings

Tibesta Manor House, Grampound
16thC wall painting remnants

St Clement's Churchtown, Near Truro

ST. CLEMENTS CHURCHTOWN
& TRESILLIAN RIVER

12.9.'92

J oanna Mattingly is a visual historian, interested in mediaeval churches, houses and museum artefacts. She studied history at the University of London. She has written, published and advised on many aspects of local and architectural history, including a recent guide to the churches of Cornwall. Dr Mattingly has just completed *Cornwall and the Coast - Mousehole and Newlyn* for the *Victoria County History of Cornwall*. Sketching is an integral part of her research. She is married and lives in Truro.

Photo: Martha Carlin

Stephen Tyrrell

Stephen Tyrrell has designed for and worked in the restoration of buildings for many years. A member of the Institute of Historic Building Consultants, he is enthusiastic about buildings and their history. His next in a series of books on architectural history, *Early Decorative Plasterwork of Cornwall,* is eagerly awaited. Stephen Tyrrell lives near Falmouth with an understanding wife.

Both Dr Mattingly and Stephen Tyrrell are members of the *Cornish Buildings Group*.